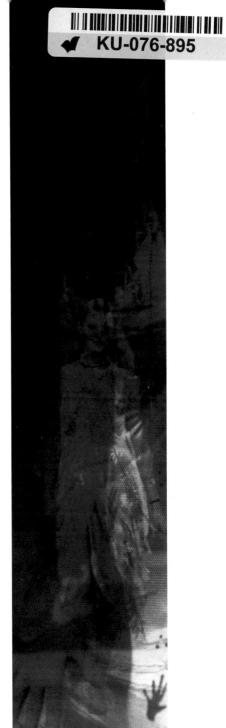

Claudia Schiffer in the Bvlgari fashion show in Basel, held during Watch and Jewelry Fair. She is wearing a necklace from the *Bvlgari Collection Internationale*, an *Ovale* watch and the *Trika* and *Nuvole* bracelets.

On the occasion of the traditional Watch and Jewelry Fair in Basel in 1999, Bvlgari organized an original fashion show with fifteen international top models. Led by Claudia Schiffer, the models were dressed entirely from the Bvlgari silk and cashmere collections. Stoles, shawls and scarves were transformed into outfits of sharp colors and elegant lines, and all of these were enhanced by jewels, leather accessories, watches, eyewear and other articles from the *Bvlgari Collection Internationale*.

BVLGARI

BVLGARI

LEONARDO ARTE

E

The Basel Fashion Show

Anna Maria Cseh wearing scarves from the *Tribale* silk collection, a Bvlgari handbag and sunglasses, *Celtaura* and *Parentesi* bracelets and an *Ovale* watch.

Top model Gretha Cavazzoni wearing scarves from the *Tribale* silk collection, *Spiga* bracelets and an *Ovale* watch.

Claudia Schiffer with a necklace from the *Bvlgari Collection Internationale*, an *Ovale* watch and the *Trika* and *Nuvole* bracelets.

BV

New Jewelry

XL, launched in 1997, is a new line of rings characterized by mass and exuberant design. The forms are inspired by a tendency to the bulky, and have a powerful visual impact. The extraordinary sense of volume in the *Piramide* ring is the result of original settings combined with the most varied materials—from colored cabochon to heart-shaped stones, with diamonds either cut for brilliance or set *à pavé*.

Piramide rings from the *XL* collection in white gold with black onyx and diamonds *pavé*.

Elizabeth Hurley wearing a *Piramide* ring.

Carrie Ann Moss, female lead in the film *The Matrix*, wearing the *Stalattite* necklace from the *Bvlgari Collection Internationale.*

Leading features of the recent collections have been classic design and attention to the effects of reflected white light. This can be seen in the platinum *Stalattite* necklace, with its pendant of eight oval diamonds diminishing in size. The new parures bring together gold, diamonds and pearls to illuminate sophisticated works of jewelry that are intended as an expression of a discrete yet determined femininity.

The *Stalattite* necklace, part of the *Bvlgari Collection Internationale*.

B.zero 1 is a fun new ring that is designed to embody an end-of-the-millennium luxury which is both spare and universal, which brings together opposites. In effect, *B.zero 1* aims to express both the beginning and the culmination, the past and the present, of Bvlgari's adventure in creation — an adventure which has always centered on unmistakable style and constant attention to the future.

B.zero 1 rings in yellow gold.

Advertising campaign for the *B.zero 1* rings in white gold designed by Fabrizio Ferri.

Anjelica Huston tries on a *B.zero 1* at the opening of the newly restructured store on Via dei Condotti in Rome.

The celebrities who have fallen in love with the *B.zero1*: Maria Grazie Cucinotta, Melba Ruffo di Calabria, Lady Helen Taylor, Lauryn Hill, Claudia Schiffer, Courtney Cox, Whitney Houston, Michelle Yoeh, Tracee Ross, Anjelica Huston, Naomi Campbell, Saffron Aldridge, Maria Bartiromo and Renato Zero.

"I really was especially grateful to be given the new ring which I haven't yet taken off!" (Lady Helen Taylor); "I have not taken the ring off my finger. It went to an In Style party, the MTV Awards, Glamour party. My finger was looking gorgeous." (Tracee Ross); "Thank you so much for getting the stunning ring for me, I love it and it only leaves my hands to go to sleep. I wear it on my middle finger and it certainly looks very cool, in fact I have had a mountain of compliments from both men and women about it so I'm very happy." (Saffron Aldridge)

Renato Zero tries on a *B.zero 1* at the launch of the restructured store in Rome.

Pigna necklace and earrings.

The *Pigna* parure is inspired by the classic motifs of Indian jewelry: white gold and diamonds enhanced with the magical gleam of pearls.

In the *Pagoda* parure the geometrical lozenges set amidst harmonious curves exalt the impact produced by the combination of white gold and *pavé* diamonds.

Pagoda necklace and earrings.

Lady Helen Taylor wearing a *Tubini* necklace.

Catherine Zeta Jones wearing the *Nuvole* parure at the London premiere of the film *The Mask of Zorro*.

Drew Barrymore at the Cinderella's Ball Party, wearing a necklace in white gold with a single, center-mounted, Ceylon sapphire of 110.76 carats, Rome.

Sharon Stone with Elton John and Elizabeth Hurley at the Cannes Film Festival. Sharon Stone is wearing a *Trika* watch and *Trika* and *Nuvole* bracelets.

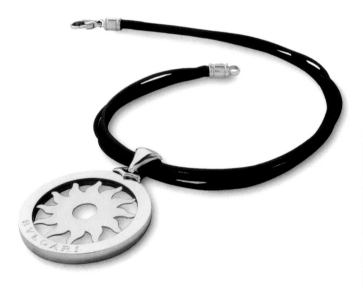

Tondo pendant from the *XL* collection in yellow gold and steel.

The top model Iman wearing a *Tondo* pendant from the *XL* collection, New York.

Veronica Webb, wearing a *Tondo* pendant from the *XL* collection, together with Nicola Bulgari.

Courtney Cox wearing a *Tondo* pendant and a mini shoulder bag in satin.

Diamonds are Forever

Donatella Versace, Kate Moss, Naomi Campbell and other models at the Diamonds are Forever fashion show, celebration of the Millennium. Kate Moss is wearing the *Millennium Renaissance* headpiece created by Bvlgari for the occasion.

On June 9, 1999, Bvlgari was in London to participate at a special event held in the presence of HRH Charles, Prince of Wales and organized by Versace and De Beers: Diamonds are Forever. This celebration presented the most extraordinary diamond jewelry created for the new millennium to raise funds for three important charities.

Catherine Zeta Jones with HRH the Prince of Wales at Diamonds are Forever. She is wearing a parure from the *Bvlgari Collection Internationale.*

Rachel Griffith wearing a bracelet from the *Bvlgari Collection Internationale* at the Oscar Ceremony in Los Angeles.

For that evening, Bvlgari created *Millennium Renaissance*, an ornamental headpiece that was in some way emblematic of a renewed interest in royalty. At the same time it is a revolutionary piece of jewelry: a combination of diadem and earrings, comprising a band of white gold set with more than two hundred and fifty diamonds. Designed for the future yet reminiscent of a past of grace and femininity, *Millennium Renaissance* is an original and daring piece of jewelry. Highlighting the beauty of the most precious of stones in an almost provocative way, it stands as the unchallenged symbol of third millennium luxury.

Millennium Renaissance photographed by Albert Watson: 253 diamonds, completed at either end by two spectacular yellow diamonds of approximately 29 carats each.

Madonna wearing a parure of gold and diamonds from *Bvlgari Collection Internationale* at the premiere of the film *Evita*.

Charlize Theron wearing a diamond bracelet from the *Bvlgari Collection Internationale* at the Golden Globe Awards Ceremony, Los Angeles.

1

Watches

Chrono watch in steel with black and white face. The watch has an automatic movement and is complete with chronograph and date.

Van Kilmer wearing a *Chrono* watch in a scene from the film *The Saint*.

Ridley Scott wearing a *Scuba Chrono*, Rome.

Sting wearing a *Bvlgari-Bvlgari* watch.

Kate Capshaw with Steven Spielberg at the premiere of the film *Saving Private Ryan*. Kate Capshaw is wearing a *Bvlgari-Bvlgari* watch and a *Tubogas* bracelet.

Bvlgari-Bvlgari watch with a *Tubogas* "serpent" bracelet in steel.

1999 saw a rediscovery of diamonds, and Bvlgari used this most precious of stones to enhance some of its classic watches, such as *Bvlgari-Bvlgari, Anfiteatro, Quadrato* and *Sport*, with sparkling *pavé* diamonds being used to decorate faces and hands. Following upon the extraordinary success of the famous *Tubogas* model with its "serpent" bracelet in gold, Bvlgari presented a steel version, with the characteristic spirals wrapping around the wrist.

Claudia Schiffer wearing a *Quadrato* watch.

For Bvlgari the passage of time means precious materials, advanced technology and, of course, elegance. This is the spirit behind the 1998 *Aluminium*, a simple, stream-lined watch that draws on new technologies of design and construction without in any way abandoning aesthetic delight. In fact, *Aluminium* stands out for its daring use of materials, whose expressive potential is exploited to the full through the original and imaginative juxtaposition of rubber and aluminum — futuristic gleams and natural flexibility. The watch was immediately a great success, with orders coming in from clients all over the world.

Aluminium Chrono watch with an aluminum body, machine-grey face and an aluminum and rubber strap. The watch has an automatic movement, and is complete with chronograph and date.

Paolo Bulgari with the jumbo jet in the background.

In the very year it was launched *Aluminium* was the center of a very special event. Following an agreement between Bvlgari and Alitalia, for one whole year the colors of the *Aluminium* line formed the livery of a Boeing 747 of the Italian Airlines, flying on the intercontinental routes between Italy, the United States, South America, the Far East and Australia. "Bvlgari flies with Alitalia" was the effective slogan which appeared on the fuselage, aptly summing up an exceptional collaboration that provided a remarkable testimonial for one of Bvlgari's most popular watches. It was the first time that a company operating in the luxury goods sector had chosen this "customization" of an airline plane to advertise the launch of one of its products. However, this original union of these two apparently distinct objects should come as no surprise. Lean and incisive in design, *Aluminium* conveys an idea of forward-looking power thanks to its daring synthesis of "technological" materials in the expression of a hi-tech concept—something one might say about the Boeing 747 itself.

Ovale is designed for the discrete femininity of the contemporary woman. Its characteristic feature is a clear and harmonious line, which brings out all the essence of the precious gold and diamonds.

Ovale watches in white gold, with or without diamonds on the body and the *réhaut*, with lizardskin strap.

Anfiteatro watch with diamonds.

Michelle Yeoh and Pierce Brosnan at the premiere of the James Bond film *Tomorrow Never Dies*. Michelle Yeoh is wearing a *Trika* watch and *Stalattite* earrings.

Sport watch with diamonds.

Alessandro Gassman in Rome, wearing a *Solo tempo* watch.

Carlo Verdone wearing a *Sport* watch and *Eccentrica* sunglasses.

Antonio Banderas wearing an *Aluminium* watch.

Naomi Campbell with an *Aluminium* watch at the Louis Vuitton party in New York.

'L

Costume Designers Guild Awards

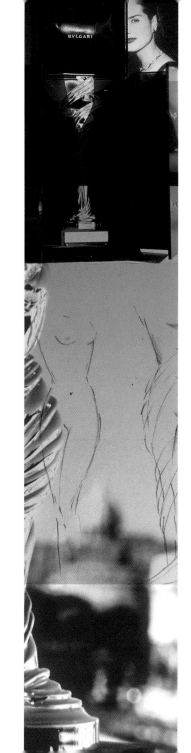

The silver statuette created by Bvlgari for the Costume Designers Guild Awards, intended to celebrate the great talents and successes among the costume designers working in cinema and television.

Of all the companies that presented designs for the future award, the Guild chose Bvlgari, immediately fascinated by the imaginative form of its sinuous and smoothly-finished statuette, in which one can see elements of the neo-classical mixed together with the magic of 1940s Hollywood.

Nicola Bulgari with Inés Sastre and Brooke Shields at the Costume Designers Guild Awards ceremony. Brooke Shields is wearing a *Nuvole* parure in platinum and diamonds.

On February 6, 1999, the Costume Designers Guild, founded in 1953 by a group of thirty cinema designers, held its first Costume Designers Guild Awards, intended to celebrate the talent and work of the best of the world's costume designers. The Mistress of Ceremonies was Anjelica Huston, assisted by a galaxy of stars including Annette Bening, Inés Sastre, Holly Hunter and Brooke Shields.

Preparatory designs for the Bvlgari statuette.

Silk and Cashmere Accessories

Scarves in *Pascolo rupestre* silk georgette from the *Tribale* collection of silk accessories.

Tribale takes us into a distant world that stirs the imagination of one and all. Using silk, cashmere and other precious materials, this 1999 *Tribale* collection by Bvlgari takes up the evocative traces of the tribal world and reworks them using imagination and memory to create a line of products which express a world that is both very distant from and very close to that of contemporary taste. The cheerful silk twills, transparent georgette, ample chiffon, precious cashmere and fine linens, evoke feelings and memories which, through magically nuanced color and design, are rendered in light, impalpable textiles. The very themes of the *Tribale* collection are reflected in the names of the pieces: *Pioggia di boomerang, Danza zebrata, Laguna, Impronte, Ritratto* and *Pascolo rupestre*.

Scarves in *Passeggiata* silk georgette from the *Tribale* collection of silk accessories.

"February" in the calendar created by Fabrizio Ferri for Bvlgari for the launch of the *Tribale* silkwear collection.

The launch of *Tribale* was accompanied by the release of an exclusive calendar, in which the eye and lens of Fabrizio Ferri caught the archetypal features of the collection, revealing the characteristic colors and motifs of places remote in time and space. The sensitive response of the photographer gives a magic rendering of the designs of *Tribale*, as his lens captures the slow and sensual movements of dancers whose painted bodies seem to bring the motifs to life.

"July" in the calendar created by Fabrizio Ferri for Bvlgari.

Balanced between reality and imagination, the Bvlgari creations conjure up an atmosphere of mystery and evocation, of intensity and beauty. Like the tattooed memories of the woman of today, they gleam from the depths of blackness as light out of the dark.

"December" in Fabrizio Ferri's Bvlgari calendar.

The International launch of *Tribale* at Industria Superstudio, New York, in November 1998. Detail of the display.

Bvlgari sets out on a creative adventure; and its course can be charted amidst the fragments of a primitive portrait drawn on a cliff face or in the footprints which disappear across empty Savannah. This world — in which the dance of the Masai echoes in the distance while magical rain obeys the ritual boomerang — is rendered in the vibrant and nuanced tones of Davide Pizzigoni's watercolors.

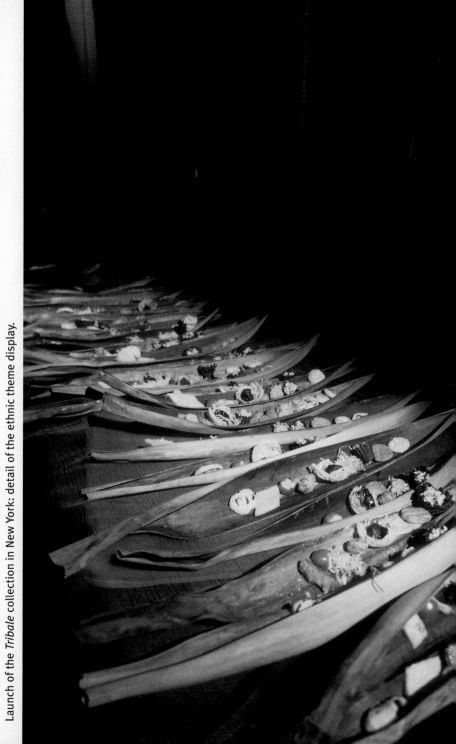

Launch of the *Tribale* collection in New York: detail of the ethnic theme display.

Francesco Trapani (CEO of the Bvlgari Group) with Tracee Ross, among the other guests taking part in the *Tribale* collection festivities.

Francesco Trapani with Donald Trump during the New York launch.

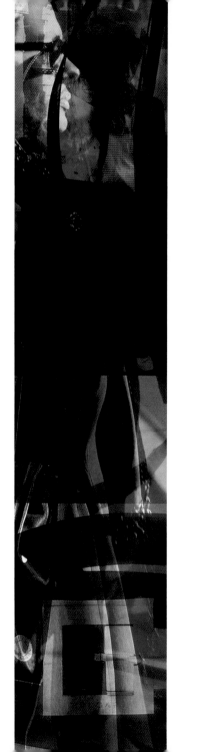

71

Leather Accessories

Shoulder bag in nylon and black leather, with four expanding sections and palladium fastener, from the first leather collection. The shoulder bag is modeled on the traditional satchel of the Italian postman, with the individual compartments for personal belongings.

In 1997 Bvlgari launched its first collection of leather accessories, comprising handbags and other small leather items. Original yet discrete elegance, innovation, rigorous and modern lines, functional design—these were some of the features of a collection that was in perfect harmony with all the various needs of modern life. Both the appearance and practical nature of each product was clearly the result of a careful process of development.

Claudia Schiffer with a shoulder bag walking on Madison Avenue, New York.

Image from the Fabrizio Ferri advertising campaign for the launch of the first leatherwear collection.

Given the variety of client requirements, Bvlgari has opted to use a wide range of material and forms — from the expanding bags that are rather like postmen's satchels to "back-packs" and the precious handbags in Louisiana crocodile. But there is one common denominator: a style so modern that it is destined to become a classic.

Melba Ruffo di Calabria with Bvlgari black handbag, Naples.

Maria Grazia Cucinotta with a Bvlgari shopping bag, a *Chrono* watch and a *Piramide* ring from the XL collection.

All Bvlgari leather goods are handmade by Italian craftsmen, using best-quality leather that has been tanned using special techniques that enhance the grain.
The use of such special materials as black leather, embossed amber leather, or black and honey-colored crocodile—together with the adoption of a contemporary design that plays on motifs of easily recognizable square lines—all this produces a vast range of high-quality, versatile pieces that are designed for a demanding and sophisticated public.

Woman's belt in black leather with a square buckle in palladium, from the first leatherwear collection.

r A

Eyewear

Aluminium eyeglasses in aluminum and acetate, with special case, from the 1999 collection of men and women's eyewear.

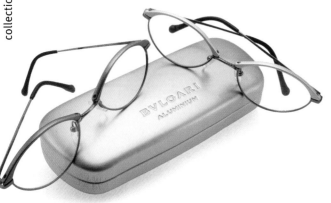

In 1999 Bvlgari research led to the creation of *Aluminium*, a new series of aluminum frames, which took up the material that had been used for the watch of the same name. Lines became even thinner; and in its use of such a light metal—a very synthesis of the classic and the original—Bvlgari seemed to take up the challenge of producing invisible eyewear.

In 1997 Bvlgari presented its first collection of eyeglasses. As with all its accessories, this eyewear collection (prescription and sunwear) was designed to meet the demands of a public that requires functionality and not just fashion.

Image from Fabrizio Ferri's advertising campaign for the men and women's collection of sunglasses.

Sheryl Crow wearing a *Bvlgari-Bvlgari* watch, a *Tubogas* bracelet, a ring with an antique coin and sunglasses from the *Eccentrica* line.

Bvlgari eyewear is the result of research intended to bring together form and content—that is, which can combine truly functional design and unmistakable style. The result is a collection characterized by innovative design and careful attention to details, which exploits a wide variety of forms and different materials—ranging from acetate through steel and titanium to 18-carat gold.

AI

Black

Bvlgari's latest contribution to the fragrance world is *Black*, a perfume for men and women which is intended as an expression of the global, metropolitan spirit of our age. Designed to be worn, experienced and admired, *Black* goes beyond any of the usual pyramids of scent combinations, given that all the essences that compose it form a single block dominated by the scent of black Lapsang tea.

In both the scent itself and the packaging, each single feature is direct and incisive.

The design of the bottle is inspired by Zen minimalism, by the principles of harmony in form and proportion that are typical of the Orient. Thanks to the contrast of materials — rubber and steel, translucid glass and cold metal — the bottle stimulates the sense of touch as well as that of sight.

Boy George at the launch of *Black*, at the D.J.'s console of London's Vinopolis Vaults.

The bar of the Vinopolis Vaults has the same shape as the bottle of *Black*.

The hall of the Vinopolis
Vaults discotheque.

Hydra Thé Vitalisant

Bvlgari enters the world of cosmetics with its *Hydra Thé Vitalisant* line, innovative products created in collaboration with one of the most prestigious cosmetic laboratories in Japan, a country which is in the very avant-garde of research in this sector. The line draws its inspiration from an Oriental philosophy of life, which lays down that pleasures arise from ourselves, from our respect for our own rhythms, our attentiveness to our desires. These principles of Oriental medicine are complemented by the latest technological advances in natural skin care and rejuvenation, exploiting all the therapeutic powers of green tea in antioxidizing, protecting and regenerating skin cells.

The *Hydra Thé Vitalisant* cosmetics.

The dining room during the launch of the *Hydra Thé Vitalisant* line in Milan.

Part of the display.

R]

Home Designs

Home Designs is a complete collection of articles for the home, in fine porcelain, crystal and silver. The range is characterized by its sober and elegant design, high-quality materials and use of avant-garde technology. It comprises two table services, one coffee and tea service, a set of solid silver cutlery, a series of table glasses, bar glasses and a selection of gift items – boxes, ashtrays, candelabras, vases. For the production, Bvlgari relied on the indisputable experience of the historic firm of Rosenthal, one of the most prestigious porcelain and glassware producers in the world.

Views of the display in the Bvlgari store on Via della Spiga, Milan, for the Italian press launch of the first *Home Designs* collection.

Photo by Fabrizio Ferri for the launch of the first *Home Designs* collection.

Porcelain is the fine basis for the decorations inspired by Davide Pizzigoni's watercolors, which provide two of the themes in the collection: *Frutta alla finestra*, in which a variety of richly-colored fruit is seen framed within a framework of blue or gold tracery and *Quadri*, in which the edges are finished with geometrical motifs in gold or black.

Selection of *Frutta alla finestra* plates in fine porcelain, from the first *Home Designs* collection.

The *Quadri* table service.

The *Dolci déco* range.

Selection of *Pascolo rupestre* furnishings.

Tondo bar glasses from the first *Home Designs* collection.

A quality accompaniment for this porcelain is Bvlgari crystalware, combining elegance of form with advanced technological know-how. The *Eccentrica* line comprises four crystal wine glasses that would enhance any table. The collection of crystalware is completed by the *Tondo* line, four types of bar glass in which the transparency of the crystal in the upper part contrasts with the sand-treated "frosted" glass of the base.

Bvlgari Stores

New York, the restructured Fifth Avenue store.

After extensive restructuring work, the Bvlgari store on Fifth Avenue reopened in 1997. Thus the Big Apple now has its own Bvlgari "flagship." Destined to become one of the most famous shopping spaces in the world, the new store has almost double the floor space, spread over two levels. The second floor is dedicated entirely to accessories—perfumes, silkwear, leatherwear and eyeglasses—as well as housing the Bvlgari Café, which offers visitors the chance to enjoy a real Italian coffee. The aim of the new store is to charm visitors not only with the splendor of Bvlgari jewelry but also with this exclusive piece of interior design, which for all its innovation remains faithful to the materials and traditions of Italian architecture.

Jeddah.

San Francisco.

Paris, Avenue Montaigne.

Las Vegas.

Tokyo,
Ginza Bridal Saloon.

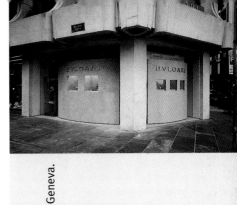

Geneva.

Twenty-five years ago Bvlgari chose Geneva as the first stepping-stone on its worldwide adventure. Now, after its refitting, that historic store is the symbol of the "label" at the beginning of the new millennium. To commemorate the event, Bvlgari produced a special limited edition of its classic watch *Bvlgari-Bvlgari*, in steel with a white or silver face — and a transparent encasement revealing all the workings of its automatic movement.

Tokyo Kioicho.

Brussels.

Sydney,
Castelreagh Street.

Sylt.

Venice.

After Rome, Milan, Florence and Cortina, in 1998 Bvlgari opened its fifth Italian store in Venice, a junction between East and West. Situated in the San Marco district, the space offers the public seven store windows and an elegant interior designed around a combination of pink marble and pearwood. The perfect setting to admire Bvlgari jewelry and accessories.

The new store on Via della Spiga in Milan after its recent restructuring.

The ninth store opened by the Roman jewelers, in the old city center of Bologna, nestling among medieval palaces and arcaded streets.

Bologna.

Padua.

A few months later Bvlgari arrived in Naples, with an exclusive store that marked the company's first launch southwards, in an area where such "names" were missing. As was befitting in a city known for its creative and vital energy, Bvlgari opted for a high-profile site of architectural importance, within the Art Nouveau complex of Palazzo Mannaiuolo.

Naples.

The new store in Mexico City is our first sales point in Latin America, where Bvlgari has for some time now been a significant presence with a very faithful clientele. The imposing architecture of the building chosen brings together the classic style of Bvlgari with the Aztec heritage of Mexico. At the opening of the store, Claudia Schiffer was the guest of honor.

Claudia Schiffer with the Bvlgari bag, created especially for her, at the Mexico City opening.

Nicola Bulgari together with Claudia Schiffer at the ribbon-cutting ceremony of the Bvlgari store in Mexico City. Claudia Schiffer is wearing a platinum, pearl and diamond necklace from the *Bvlgari Collection Internationale.*

Sketch of new facade of the Via dei Condotti store, Rome.

1999 saw the total renovation of the original Bvlgari store at number 10, Via dei Condotti. Opened in 1905 by Sotirio Bulgari, the founder of the company, the store had previously been renovated in the 1930s.

Part of the Renaissance Palazzo Lepri, the store was extended to obtain much more sales and display area. The entire work of restructuring aimed to maintain as much of the original materials and style as possible—even here, revealing Bvlgari's desire to bring together tradition and innovation.

Precious woods—such as pear, maple, cherry and walnut—have been used in the fittings for a store that will now have not only its traditional jewelry section but also departments for new Bvlgari lines, such as silk and leatherwear accessories and eyewear. An entire room is dedicated to the new *Homes Designs* line of porcelain, crystal and silverware for the home.

The new layout has also created space for the "Silver Gallery," which houses Bvlgari's famous collection of antique silver.

The reopening of the historic Bvlgari store on Via dei Condotti was a mondaine event that attracted celebrities from the world of art and show business. Held in the special atmosphere of the pre-Christmas period, this exclusive vernissage was an original way of reliving the heyday of the Rome's *La Dolce Vita*. Among the friends and faithful clients present were Susanna Agnelli, Giorgio Forattini, Francesco Rutelli and Barbara Palombelli, Renato Zero, Monica Vitti and Roberto Russo, Christian De Sica, Valeria Bruni Tedeschi, Enrico Vanzina, Athina Cenci, Marisa Laurito, Monica Scattini, Roberto D'Agostini, Egon von Furstenberg, Gianna Letta, Fabio Capello, Giovanni Malagò, Guido Torlonia and many others.

View of the store on Via dei Condotti, Rome, after restructuring.

Room within the new section of the Via dei Condotti store dedicated to the *Home Designs* collection.

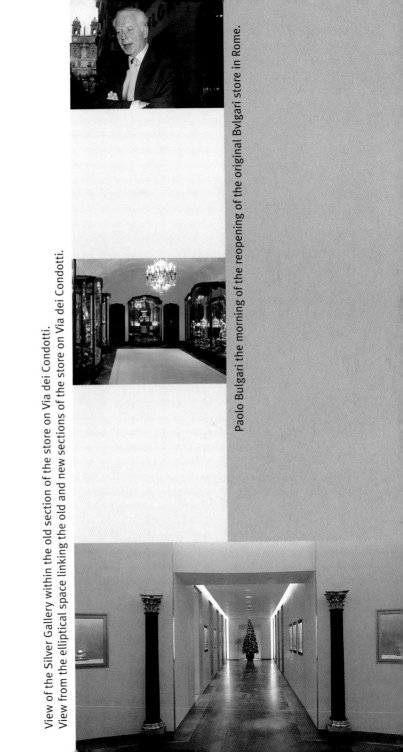

View of the Silver Gallery within the old section of the store on Via dei Condotti.
View from the elliptical space linking the old and new sections of the store on Via dei Condotti.

Paolo Bulgari the morning of the reopening of the original Bvlgari store in Rome.

Cartoonist Giorgio Forattini and Paolo Bulgari.

Susanna Agnelli and Paolo Bulgari.

Enrico Lo Verso.

Lady Helen Taylor, Tim Taylor, Nicola Bulgari and Francesco Trapani.

Christian De Sica.

Monica Vitti.

Text by Marina Rotondo

English Translation
Jeremy Scott

Special Thanks to

Bvlgari Corporate External Relations
Sabina Guerrieri

Photographers
David Bailey, Nelly Bellati, Alex Berliner, Federico Brunetti,
Umberto Buzzacchi, Ottavio Celestino, Curti & Parini, Marco Delogu,
Europa Press Service, Fabrizio Ferri, Massimo Fossati, Volker Frenzel,
Francesco Garufi, Claude Joray, Minoru Karamatu, Simon Kenny,
Lo Studiolo, Salvatore Mancuso, Marco Marianella, Fabio Meazzi,
Monzino, Stephen Morley, Antonio Mulas, Fotocronache Olimpia,
Oriani & Origone, Studio Orizzonte, Rosenthal AG, Vittorio Sacco,
Shinichi Sato, Carl Saytor, Marco Scarpa, Studio Sclavi, Germàn Silva,
Stefano Uvietta, Dirk Vogel, Albert Watson, Richard Young

Magazines
Detour Magazine, Hello!, Mademoiselle, Sun Herald Newspaper,
Vogue Germany, WWD

Holders of rights to any unidentified photographic material are invited to
bring the matter to the attention of the originating publishers, Leonardo Arte.

This volume was printed on behalf of Elemond S.p.a.
at Martellago Mondadori Printing S.p.a.,
Via Castellana 98, Martellago (Venice) in the year 2000